The Greatest Little Transformation Book You'll Ever Read!

by John Brady ❖ Timothy Smith

COPYRIGHT © 1995 JBA PRESS.

All Rights Reserved. No part of this report may be reproduced, recreated, reimagined, or transmitted in any form or by any means, electronic, mechanical, atomic, subatomic, physical, or metaphysical, including photocopying, faxing, recording, daytime talk shows, telepathy, or channeling. Neither can it be stored in information storage and retrieval systems, planetary, interplanetary, galactic and/or intergalactic, blah, blah, blah, and so forth, without written permission from the Big Kahuna at JBA Press.

FINE PRINT: IF YOU'VE ACTUALLY READ THIS FAR, YOU'LL PROBABLY COPY WHAT YOU WANT ANYWAY. JUST REMEMBER WHERE YOU GOT IT. THANKS.

Library of Congress Cataloging-in-Publication Data

Brady, John
   The best little transformation book you'll ever read! / John Brady and Timothy Smith.--1st ed.

   Bibliography: p.
   ISBN 0-9649230-5-X
     1. Organizational effectiveness. 2. Organizational transformation.
I. Smith, Timothy. II. Title
HD58.9.B51   1995
658.4--dc19   95-92025
                                                           CIP

This book was edited by Clare Silvestri.

Additional copies are available from:

JBA Press, P.O. Box 772
San Luis Obispo, California 93406
805 549-8246 ▲ FAX 805 549-0339

WARNING–This little book could change your life! It has been known to cause spontaneous insight about transformation. It may challenge your perception of reality, and even make you ponder, laugh, say 'hmmm,' and scratch your head in wonder or disbelief. What the heck, what's life without risk anyway?   --JBA Press

ACKNOWLEDGMENTS

Mange Takk...Thanks A Million...Arigatō... Mil Gracias...Merci!...Hartelijk Dank...Grazie...

The Greatest Little Transformation Book is not an original work, but a synthesis of great ideas by great change agents. We've borrowed liberally from credible people who've been on the leading edge of major change.

This is a "do-it" book with a definite point of view. You won't find wiggle words like "maybe," "kind of," or "theoretically" here. For us, transformation is a necessity, not just a trendy idea. As change agents, we live and work in the world of transformation every day. Our point of view is, *"Transform now or be transformed later."*

Transformation can be serious business, but it doesn't have to be somber, so we throw in humor wherever possible. We're grateful for the thoughts and writings of the great transformers like Frank Brady, Rege Filtz, Tom Peters, Pogo, Alvin Toffler, Toyoo Gyohten, Yoda, Ray Smith, John Otter, James Heskett, Lao Tsu, Chris Argryis, Edgar Schein, Pinocchio, Price Pritchett, Buddy Holly, Al Morrison, John Naisbitt, Li'l Abner, John Heider, Peter Senge, R. Beckhard, Pooh Bear, Joe Romano, R. Harris, Ralph Kilmann, Pecos Bill, James Cribbin, Larry Miller, Siddhartha Gautama, Terence Deal, Alley Oop, Allan Kennedy, Bill Ferguson, Roy Rogers, and Gary Larson who are the fountains of wisdom from which this book flowed.

Life is a transforming path. This is our way of checking in with you while we travel the path. We'd like to hear how your travels are going, too.

We also thank *you* for choosing this little book and your willingness to consider our view of Transformation.

Table of Contents

Prologue--Danger or Opportunity? 1

The Bottom-Line 4

Transformation Is A Choice? 10

Hot Culture = Hot ROI 16

Cooperation or Annihilation 21

Transformation Busters 27

Transformation = Trophy 33

Using "Outsider Eyes" 47

Experienced Consultant/Coach/Change Agents 54

Endnotes 56

*"In stable times, everything had a name
and everything knew its place, and individuals
could affect very little.*

*Now, we live in an era of 'transformation,'
and we have extraordinary personal leverage
and personal influence..."*

--Alvin Toffler, paraphrase

1
Prologue--
Transformation, Danger or Opportunity?

The Chinese 危机 pictograph for crisis and transformation 危机 is a combination of two characters: "danger" and "opportunity."[1] That's what is facing us today with organizational transformation.

Some see this change as danger, others as opportunity. We see it as both, simultaneously. It's only human to avoid risk, even at the expense of missing valuable opportunities.

Today, leaders often look at transformation as an insurmountable obstacle to be quickly gotten through, around, or hurdled over. If we listen to the wisdom of Chinese sages, we learn transformation is an <u>opportunity when we face it</u>, and <u>danger when we try to avoid it</u>.

Our Promise to you...

This little book is a quick read. It's the "Poor Richard's Almanac" of transformation books--it's guaranteed to contain no mumbo-jumbo, no gobbledygook--only:

1. Straight forward principles and methodologies to bring about meaningful, long lasting change, and

2. Methods to manage the human fabric of organizational life for long-term success.

We've written this book for real leaders facing the realities of transforming their companies. It starts where most of the big, best-selling management books leave off, and supplies what the "number cruncher" approaches to transformation overlook-- common sense.

How Do We Know?

Like Red Adair, who spends his life putting out oil well fire storms, we spend our lives in the storms of organization change. We're the Red Adairs of corporate transformation. It's all we do. We help organizations transform the ambiguity, uncertainty, and ambivalence of change into positive bottom-line results.

This Little Transformation *book will tell you how we do it...*

Last Things First . . .

"If you have anything of importance to tell me, for Pete's sake, begin at the end."

--SARA JEANETTE DUNCAN

2
The Bottom-Line

The bottom-line about change is face it and grow, or be changed by circumstances beyond your control. Survival, success, and satisfaction in the future require that every person and organization transform themselves into adaptive, motivated dynamos.

What's Driving All This Change?

Tom Peters, the guru of transformation, tells this story on himself that illustrates the very nature of the speed of changing times:

> *"My own ignorance about the increasing pace of change was bluntly pointed out to me when I purchased a laptop computer. After a bit of study, I settled on a cutting-edge model. I brought it home and proudly showed it to my son. 'That,' he sneered, ' is the <u>old</u> one. I think it's been out four or five months.' He was right. It <u>was</u> an old one -- an antique at age 120 days. It has already been discontinued."*[2]

If Tom Peters is surprised, we should be astonished. Not just about the computer, but how it represents the cause and effect of the blinding speed of change.

There were 2.3 million low-tech computers in 1980 compared to more than 90 million high-tech computers today. In the last fifteen years PC/Apple-type software revenues have grown from less than $1 billion to more than $11.6 billion (Evens before Windows 95!).

So, what's the big deal? With millions of computers throwing mega-trillions of bits of information around at light speed, it takes an entirely new kind of adaptive leadership and organization to keep up. New, adaptive leaders and teams are emerging as the prime movers within successful organizations. These new adaptive leaders and teams are agile, autonomous, and quick.

Recognizing this, AT&T Chairman Robert Allen announced on September 20, 1995 that he was spinning off three viable business units, quitting the PC business, and selling his Capital company. A dozen years after the first divestiture, Divestiture-2 restructured AT&T into three major, independent businesses--communications services, communications equipment and transaction computing.

Allen said in his announcement, *"Changes in customer needs, technology and public policy are radically transforming our industry ... and we feel that the new structure will make AT&T's businesses more valuable to our shareowners, more responsive to customers, and better able to focus on the growth opportunities in their individual markets."*[3]

This stunning move drives home a message: *AT&T and many of the Fortune 500 are waking up to the fact that the nimble company with clear business aims, not a vast overarching giant, will prosper in the new business paradigm.*

Prophetically, in 1993, Texas Instruments's Steve Truett and EDS's Tom Barrett predicted, *"The lumbering bureaucracies of this century are being replaced by fluid, independent groups of problem solvers ... "*

We are literally defining a new organizational paradigm, with new ways of leading and managing them. Following are nine things you absolutely must know about the new paradigm:

Nine Things You Must Know About the Transformation:

1. Transformation Is A Choice? -- Some say transformation is a choice. Tell that to the ABC, CBS, and Turner television networks which were are the targets of mergers by Disney ($19 billion) , Westinghouse (at $5.4 billion) and Time-Warner ($7.5 billion) respectively. Tell that to AT&T Chairman Bob Allen who spent $1.5 billion to pay for splitting the company into three independent businesses.

Our view, like Disney, Westinghouse, Time-Warner and AT&T is: "transform now or be transformed later." If you as a leader choose the transformation path, you'll be taking giant strides along with the best and brightest in business today. You will also have the opportunity to create the future for yourself and your organization.

The other choice, of course, is to go slow, manage the '80s way, and following someone else who will create a future you have to adapt to.

2. Hot Culture = Hot ROI -- Creating an adaptive culture is money in the bank! Investing time, talent, and resources in the transformation process significantly fattens the bottom line, up to 750%, over ten years. How? Consider cultural ROI as *a fraction*.

Take the fraction 116/129. Phillip Morris bought Kraft for $12.9 billion, a fair price. When the CPA's finished their work, it turned out that Phillip Morris had bought $1.3 billion worth (13/129) of tangible "stuff" (assets like macaroni and cheese!), and $11.6 billion of "other." "Other" what? Intangibles! The biggest share of the purchase price, 116/129, was brand equity, and the tens of thousands of committed employees around the world--*The Kraft Culture*.

3. Cooperation or Annihilation -- Cooperation and teamwork are no longer luxuries or buzzwords in the new organization paradigm, they're requirements. You have them--you thrive; you don't--you die. And cooperation starts at the top! As the old Irish proverb says, *"One jagged tooth strips a whole gear."* A united organization is the key to success.

4. Overcoming Transformation Busters -- Thomas Kuhn, writing in *The Structure of Revolutions* said, *"Every significant breakthrough is a 'break-with'."*[4] Break-withs creates psychological shockwaves at every level of the organization, and these are transformation busters. It's a new way of thinking, feeling, and doing. Not surprisingly, some people find it constructive and some destructive.

5. Transformation = Trophy -- The Greeks used the word trope (English = trophy) to symbolize a critical turning point in a battle of arms or wits. Taking decisive action on a few key issues signals your organization that you have chosen your trophy, or turning point and there is no turning back.

Action One: *Outlaw the "quick-fix."* Transformation is a long-term, organization-wide proposition. Be understanding but firm, solutions will be long-term or not at all.

Action Two: *Set up a simple, but effective multi-track transformation process. Insist that focuses on all operational and cultural areas of the organization.* The tracks in this process address organizational culture, leadership/management skills, team building, strategy and structure, reward systems, and more.

6. Transformational Leadership -- Keeping 'on track' requires unwavering, strong commitment by the top leadership. Without leadership commitment, transformation won't work--period! Top-down commitment is the fuel of transformation. Every ship needs a captain; every plane a pilot. No less a leader than Mahatma Gahndi said, *"You must be the change you want to see."*

There is an old saying that goes, *"Nothing will be attempted if all possible objections must first be overcome."* The transformational leader's job is to lead people inspite of uncertainty, and do it by "walking the talk." In *Hanta Yo*, Ruth Beebe-Hill's book about a Lakota Sioux leader, she wrote, *"Some will say he is a messenger... I say he is the message."*

7. Using "Outsider Eyes" -- Ralph Waldo Emerson said, *"The field cannot well be seen from within the field."* This is especially true when you are dealing with corporate culture and transformation. Selecting the right consultant/coach/change agent is critical to the success of the change effort.

The coach must:
- ☞ Be at your planning table from Day One,
- ☞ Be independent and provide unbiased judgements.
- ☞ Balance business and people needs during the transformation process,
- ☞ Tell you what you don't want to hear, and
- ☞ Open your eyes when you're blind (about yourself, your team, and your total organization).

8. No Half Measures -- Remember, you and your senior team have to transform yourselves to transform your organization. It takes nerve. We all know the state of American Railroads in the '80s. Former Union Pacific Railroad boss Mike Walsh told his lieutenants to take a "clean-sheet-of-paper" approach to transformation.

Results: Walsh initiated a 120-day revolution that scraped 120 years of rust off the Union Pacific iron horse. He counsels, *"Peg the needle all the way over." "Because*," he adds, *"organizations want to take on more than their leaders give them credit for."*

9. True Grit -- Transforming your company is a classic good news/bad news story--it's unbelievably tough and it pays off big time.
- ✓ It's hard work.
- ✓ It takes guts, time, effort, resources.
- ✓ There's no short cuts, gimmicks, excuses.
- ✓ There are always setbacks--They're part of the transformation game.
- ✓ And, the **RESULTS** are worth it . . .

Subject Matter Expert

"I have travelled the length and breadth of this country, and have talked with the best people in business administration. I can assure you on the highest authority that data processing is a fad and won't last out the year."

-- Editor, Prentice-Hall circa 1957[5]

3
Transformation is a Choice?

About transformation, William Jennings Bryan said, *"Transformation is not a matter of chance, it is a matter of choice. It is not a thing to be waited for, it is a thing to be achieved."*

This report is for leaders who consciously choose to transform their organizations. It is for companies rethinking their goals and restructuring themselves. Between now and the beginning of the new millennium, leaders have an unusual window of opportunity to transform their companies into adaptive, motivated, performance-enhancing organizations.

The 'Powershifting' World

What is there about today's marketplace that creates this window of opportunity? Simply this: Smart leaders know staying ahead is better than trying to catch up. But staying ahead of what?

The Powershifting[6] world, for one. We're in the midst of a powershift which is creating a new system of wealth, and is transforming work, capital, and money itself--and therefore power. Because knowledge now provides the key raw material for wealth creation and is the new currency, the powershift has created "info wars" which have the potential for tearing the workplace apart.

We also live in a "nanosecond" era where things change at lightspeed. To complicate matters further, the organizational landscape has grown increasingly revolutionary, unstable, and unpredictable. In the tug of war between a powershifting world and the demands of nanosecond management, every organization is struggling to achieve continuous and revolutionary improvement.

What Doesn't Work...

...Panaceas which focus on a quick, simplistic, single approach. Many consultants propose these, but they fail to make a lasting difference.

Why? First, most solutions are proposed by people within the organization or consultants who were trained in the same old '70s and '80s paradigm of organizational change. They are usually blind to the solutions outside their training which create real long lasting organization change.

Second, most internal and external consultants are committed to the singular 'bread-and-butter' methodology their firm employs. An exception to this is the new A.T. Kearney Management Consultants, which recently merged with EDS to establish a comprehensive approach to finding and implementing client solutions. They are the exception. Most firms continue to use their single approach which does not create real change.

Third, many clients would rather invest in a single level quick-fix than they would a long-term multi-level change process. It's cheaper, and it gives the perception of change. Problem is, it puts the organization on a treadmill of annual programs with minimal impact on the long term results.

Today, it's obvious that single-level approaches, quick-fixes, band-aids, and magic (silver) bullets don't cut it. They fail because they don't address the total integration of the complex interrelationships of organizations.

What works?

What creates long-term organizational transformation? An integrated, multi-track approach which touches all of the critical leverage points of organizational transformation. According to Jack Welch, CEO of General Electric:

We had to undo a 100 year-old concept and convince our managers that their role is not to control people and stay 'on top' of things, but rather to guide, energize and excite. We had to convert them to the idea that we were reinventing ourselves.

The Quick and The Dead

"The nineties is a decade in a hurry," says Northern Telecom's David Vice. *"There'll be only two kinds of leaders--the quick and the dead."*

So, what's quick? Listen to this story told by Toyoo Gyohten, one-time Japanese vice minister of finance, in his book *Changing Fortunes*:

Recently, I asked one of Japan's best foreign-exchange dealers what factors he considered important to success. He answered, "I consider options that are short term, medium, and long term." I asked him what he considered long term. He paused . . . and replied with genuine seriousness, "Probably 10 minutes." That's business today.[7]

Using Organizational Leverage

The Italian economist Vilfredo Pareto's 80/20 Law states: *"20% of any cause creates 80% of any effect."*[8] In business, heads-up leaders look for and exploit the 20%, high-payoff, leverageable opportunities.

To take advantage of these high-leverage opportunities, today's leaders must transform and reinvent themselves and their entire organizations. Only an adaptive, motivated culture is agile enough to parlay high-payoff *20% opportunities into 80% payoffs*.

Albert Einstein cannily observed, *"The significant problems we face today cannot be solved at the same level of thinking we used to create them."* Adaptive leaders and their corporate cultures break the mold. As if to reply in agreement, Wayne Yetter, CEO of Astra/Merck said, *"We started with a blanksheet and drew a clear picture of who our customers are and what they want, and we are shaping our organization specifically to meet their needs."*

What Is Corporate Culture?

What exactly is corporate culture? It was once, thought to be the invention of Harvard professors trying to sell books. *"In actuality,"* Ralph Kilmann says in his book *Corporate Transformation,* *"corporate culture is like an iceberg. It is mostly invisible, quite deep, and not easily accessible. What shows above the surface--the behavioral norms or the "rules of the game"--represents that aspect of culture most easily identified and managed."* [9] According to Webster [*with some help from us] *culture* is:

> *The integrated pattern of human behavior that includes thought, speech, action, artifacts [*rites, rituals, values, norms], and embedded practices...and learning which become transmitted knowledge to succeeding generations.*

Marvin Bower, formerly managing director of McKinsey & Company and author of *The Will To Manage,* offered a more informal definition. He described corporate culture as *"the way we do things around here."*

Every business and organization has a culture. You might even call it its "personality." Organizations may also have many subcultures. Whether weak or strong, culture sets the norms for everything--from who gets promoted, what decisions are made, how employees dress, and what they do for recreation.

Culture is one of the key factors that makes or breaks transformation initiatives. It cuts both ways. John W. Teets, Chairman and CEO of the Greyhound Corporation, put it this way:

> *"It is essential for leaders to go beyond the mechanics of running the business during change. Successful leaders know getting the best results depends on minimizing cultural trauma."*

Smart leaders create an adaptive, motivated culture *before* they have to so they can stay a jump ahead of their "culturally-challenged" competitors.

Where Does Corporate Culture Fit In?

Corporate culture is one place where Pareto's 80/20 Law produces significant financial and human results. Creating a motivated corporate culture adds hard dollars to the bottom line. ✓*How much? You won't believe how much! Read on...*☞

"Winning means taking risks. You can't steal home and keep your foot on third base."

--Herbert V. Prochnow

4
Hot Culture = Hot ROI

Although baseball has fallen from grace lately, it still gives us great Return On Investment (ROI) metaphors for success. Consider the hitter:

> *Usually a hitter gets four times at bat during a game, which adds up to twelve times in three games. A .250 hitter gets three hits every twelve times at bat. A .333 hitter gets four hits every twelve times at bat. The .333 hitter gets just **one more hit** every three games. So, who cares? What's the difference?*
>
> ☞ *The .250 hitter makes **$175,000** a year* ☜
> ☞ *The .333 hitter makes **$1,500,000** a year* ☜

A winning organization is like that! Creating a culture that gets consistently better results generates huge improvements in Return On Investment. Take a look at the following short and long term payoffs.

Short Term ROI

The actual activity of change, realignment, and reorganization is usually a short term event (six months - one year). The question is, *"What impact does cultural support have on short term ROI?"*

Fact--Under the best of circumstances during the first steps of transformation a leader can only ***minimize*** the *initial dip in ROI*, and shorten its duration.

Figure 3.1

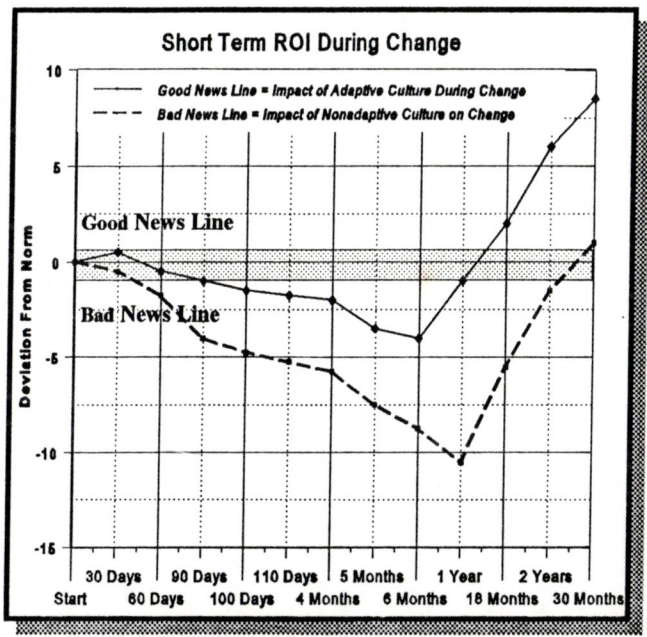

Source: John P. Kotter, James L. Heskett, Price Pritchett, and Brady & Associates

Involving the culture saves money, time, and employee good will. In Figure 3.1 above, we chart two change scenarios over a 2½ year period. The chart is based on a simple ten-point scale, representing the general patterns and shifts on ROI during the first 30 months.

Results on the top (good news) line show a transformation process that integrates all the key leverage points in the organization (culture, leadership and management skills, teamwork, strategy and structure, reward systems, and external alliances). The lower (bad news) line, traces lower results achieved by quick-fix solutions.

As consultant/coach/change agents, we've witnessed both paths first hand. Independent research by John P. Kotter, James L. Heskett[10], and Pritchett & Associates,[1]Inc. , bear out our experience. Unfortunately, most companies embark on change without consideration of creating a culture to support it, putting them on the slippery slopes of the bad news line.

17 THE GREATEST LITTLE TRANSFORMATION BOOK

Long Term ROI

Hang onto your hats, and take a look at this! John P. Kotter and James L. Heskett[9], in their book, *Corporate Culture and Performance*, published an eleven-year (1977 to 1988) study of thirty-two companies' results.

Take a moment to compare the Adaptive to the Nonadaptive Culture side-by-side, apples-to-apples in the following chart (Figure 3.2). Discover the significant quantitative differences in results between adaptive, motivated, performance-enhancing cultures and nonadaptive cultures.

Figure 3.2

LONG TERM ROI OF AN ADAPTIVE CULTURE[9]		
Key Results	Average for Twelve Firms with Adaptive, Performance-Enhancing Cultures (%)	Average for Twenty Firms with Nonadaptive, Nonperformance-Enhancing Cultures (%)
Revenue Growth 1977-88	682%	166%
Employment Growth 1977-88	282%	36%
Stock Price Growth 1977-88	901%	74%
Net Income 1977-88	756%	1%

Of the companies studied, the twelve adaptive firms stood out because they increased:

- ✓ Revenue **four times,**
  - ✓ Employment **eight times,**
    - ✓ Stock price **twelve times,** and
      - ✓ Net income **700 percent.**

Remember, these are leaders, organizations and people just like you. The 'high flying' adaptive cultures beat the competition by building committed teams empowered to deal with any challenge. They took advantage of opportunities quickly, and spotted trouble before it was a real threat. In short, they were turned-on and unbeatable.

Soft Stuff = Hard Results

Question: *Does that soft stuff make that big of a difference?*

Answer: *Definitely, Yes.* It's the same kind of soft stuff that pays baseball's .333 hitter $1.5 million and a .250 hitter $175 thousand. In baseball the 'soft stuff' might be hustle, dogged determination, mental toughness, or commitment to the team's success. In business it's things like shared vision, values, and a committed leader.

Investing in an adaptive, motivated culture is good business, very good business. *The sooner you invest in your culture, the sooner you get the bigger ROI.*

Footdraggers Law . . .

"There is nothing simple that can't be made more difficult when done with reluctance."

--Anonymous

5
Cooperation or Annihilation

The new organizational paradigm is cooperation or annihilation. The visionary Buckminster Fuller called it, *"The mysterious interaction of parts that create an unexpected greater whole--it is the secret of the universe."*

It might be mysterious, but the level of cooperation is measurable during and after transformation. Some of it is objective, and some subjective, and each carries with it its own spirit and energy.

History Lesson

From the '20s to the '70s, the autocrat reigned supreme. This was due in large part to Max Weber's theory of bureaucracy. Weber said that cooperation must be commanded and modeled after the military organization. It was an idea whose time had come and was effective in building the industrial might of the U.S. It encouraged tops-down, autocratic management styles.

All things run their course, and so it is with bureaucracy and autocracy. In the '90s and beyond they simply don't work. William Yeomans, put his finger on the death of autocracy in his "Principle of Autocratic Inaction": *"Today, the more you tell people what to do, the greater the chance they'll do it at the lowest acceptable productivity level."*[12]

Yesterday's bureaucracy and autocracy create a whole menu of what we call the *silent killers* of cooperation. These are mistrust, information "jamming," creative stalling, unwillingness to change, impaired problem-solving behaviors, and sabotage.[13]

The senior leader's role (indeed, the role of all leaders) is to build cooperation and eliminate these silent killers. One can measure cooperation on four levels. Each of the following levels has a definite, measurable impact on the profitability and velocity of transformation on the organization.

- ✔ Teamwork--Outstanding level of cooperation
- ✔ Commitment--Average level of cooperation
- ✔ Compliance--Marginal level of cooperation
- ✔ 'Pocket-Veto'--Unacceptable level of cooperation

The High-Performance Zone

The "High-Performance Zone" happens when resistance in the culture is low and velocity of change is high. It's been described by long distance runners as "being in the zone or groove."

Figure 4.1

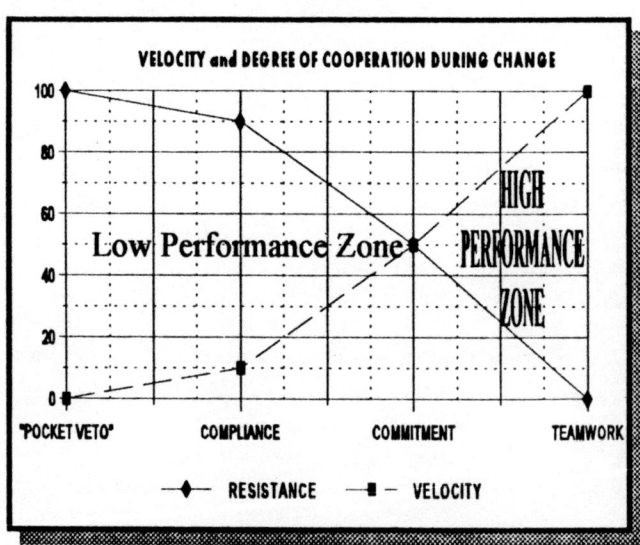

Source: Brady & Associates

The Chinese call it "wei wu wei," or doing by not doing. People in the high-performance zone pump up the organization's spirit. "In the zone," they carry out activities seamlessly with ease and grace. You can see the impact of cooperation on performance in the preceding diagram, Figure 4.1.

Charging People Up

Transformation can actually charge people up. Why? Done right, it gives them more power--they feel more control of their own destinies. Change can open doors that otherwise would remain closed to them. Change presents the leader a significant chance to harness this power and direct it into commitment.

On the other hand, change mishandled, creates resistance, and resistance is the arch enemy of commitment. *"Managing the dynamics of the reorganization process means constructively eliminating resistance and successfully managing commitment,"* says the seasoned veteran of the S&L wars, Fred W. Cover, First Texas Savings Association.

Day Late/Dollar Short

Day late and a dollar short doesn't cut in the transformation business! Here's what three companies who didn't get the message at first later said about the need for commitment and teamwork during major change:

Shering-Plough	*"Shering's people didn't adapt well. The synergism we were looking for took longer than we thought."*
Heublein-KFC	*"We learned the hard way; we made our share of mistakes; we took too long to move the culture down the learning curve."*
Squibb-Lanvin	*"We made some mistakes because we didn't understand the culture."*

Charting Your Own Course

Of course, each senior executive charts his or her own transformation course--that's what leadership is all about.

By definition, transformation is a fundamental change in strategy, structure, and nature of the organization. If these create uncertainty, people will test your resolve. You will face trials. Here's six basic guidelines to help you chart your course.

1. You and your direct reports must be committed champions of the change.

2. You must produce a "mother and apple pie" vision statement and communicate it to the organization. Along with it tell them what the new organization will look like, what its basic character will be, and what its policies, values and priorities will be.

3. Make it obvious that the status quo is dead.

4. Reinforce the fact that you're in change process for the long term, and the process is not the "program de jour."

5. Quickly reward fast starters, and discipline foot-draggers. Let the organization know you mean business.

6. Walk your talk with determination and resolve--don't hold back: No reserves, no retreats, no regrets.

Remember, you'll be tested and there will be trials. It's been said of trials, *"The brook would lose its song if it were not for the rocks in its path."* Enjoy the transformation process! It is a great adventure.

> *"A powerful tide is surging across the world today, creating a new, often bizarre, environment. We discover that many conditions that produce today's greatest perils also open fascinating new potentials."*
>
> --Alvin Toffler

6
Transformation Busters

What are they? Transformation busters are those hidden, usually untalked-about issues, that can annihilate any gain forecasted in an organizational change. And, how do you deal with them?

For starters, transformation busters aren't usually the financials or the strategy. For the most part they center around the culture. When companies change, merge or transform in other major ways the change creates *cultural shockwaves and organizational trauma*. This trauma puts a serious dent in any gain contemplated during the planning process.

Dealing with The Unknown

Most of us can remember a time in our lives as children when we were confronted with going into a dark room. For most of us, it was a traumatic moment. No matter how much encouragement and coaxing our parents gave us to go into the room, and no matter how much they urged us to trust them, we hesitated. Why? The reason for most of us was that we imagined the worst kinds of things hiding in the darkness. We say bogey men in the closet, monsters under the bed, and snakes hiding in the dark corners just waiting to bite us when we took our first step into the room.

Transformation Creates Trauma

When faced with the ambiguity created by transformation people imagine the worst, and this creates trauma. Over fifty-one percent of mergers ignore this critical issue, and over fifty-one percent of mergers fail, or fall short of their financial goals. Can you avoid or eliminate the trauma completely? No. Can you minimize it and its accompanying psychological shockwaves? Yes!

The first step to minimizing trauma and transformation shockwaves is to acknowledge them and learn to recognize their causes and symptoms. The worst thing that leaders can do during a major organization change is *ignore the trauma issues, pretend they don't exist, or hope they just go away.* Sticking your head in the sand allows three major silent killers of change to stalk your transformation process. Price Pritchett identified the following silent killers of change and symptoms of organizational trauma in his book *After the Merger: Managing the Shockwaves.*

Silent Killers of Change

Ambiguity - Change usually creates more questions than answers. People perceive a communication vacuum. There is a lack of clarity regarding the corporate future and the changes it holds. People wonder about their role in the new scheme of things.

Weakening Trust Level - Invariably, transformation, change, and reorganization cause employees to become suspicious and wary. Employees will often conclude that top management is not open and aboveboard about things.

Self-preservation - Insecurity during transformation and reorganization leads to self-preservation behaviors. The weaker the trust levels and the higher the levels of ambiguity, the more frequently self-protective behaviors surface.

Symptoms of Organizational Resistance and Trauma

When transformation busters creep through the organization, they create resistance and trauma and take a high human toll.. As this happens it wreaks havoc on profitability, productivity, and operating effectiveness.

Emotions (some visible, some invisible) begin to tangibly bias behavior, creating a kind of domino effect involving all areas of the organization. Following are six symptoms of organizational trauma which highlight top management's need to deal *quickly* and *effectively* with these transformation busters:

✓**Communication Deteriorates** - As trust levels drop, people become more closed and begin to play their cards closer to the vest. Information channels receive less dependable information. Ideas and the data submitted are more likely to be filtered, distorted, or edited completely before reaching their intended destinations.

✓**Parochialism Increases/ Team Play Deteriorates** - The transformation environment frequently freezes team play. This, of course, is an outgrowth of lower trust levels. Studies find that projects get bogged down in organizational politics. Competition subverts cooperation and the overall corporate reorganization suffers severely because of this splintering effect.[14]

✓**Power Struggles** - At best, change causes existing power networks to be reexamined and renegotiated. At worst, the situation deteriorates into a free-for-all where it's every person for him or herself. While the organization focuses internally on power issues, external competition stealthily grabs vulnerable clients and market share.

✓**Commitment Is Lost** - When uncertainty is employees' dominant reality it is difficult for them to maintain a motivated productivity. They question goals, and become preoccupied with superfluous details, and lose focus.

✓**Productivity Suffers/Momentum Sags** - Change creates uncertainty, slows decision making, and inhibits people's willingness to take risks. An air of tentativeness or a wait-and-see attitude prevails. People often move into holding patterns, deliberately choosing play-it-safe strategies.

✓**The Organization Drifts** - The overall organization begins to drift (See Figure 3-1, lower line) because it's not operating in a purposeful, coordinated effort. If there is no clear sense of direction, people become paralyzed and resources are inevitably underutilized and/or wasted completely.

✓**Sabotage and Revenge** - There is an alarming trend of unhappy employees who sabotage their organizations or take revenge on their bosses, coworkers, and company property. Their rage is often directed at the institution because they feel betrayed. At a minimum, these employees destroy or sabotage property (including computer files and management information systems), and sometimes cause injury to others and themselves.

Trauma R_x

A prescription for the transformation trauma is to involve your entire organization in the transformation process. It's good business, because they already know what changes need to be made and how to make them.

On the other hand, if people feel ignored or trampled in the transformation process, they create a serious drag on results. Transformation under these conditions would be like trying to win the America's Cup race while dragging your anchor. No chance!

In order to overcome transformation busters you must punch through the wasteland of organizational inertia. It is imperative to stay ahead of the transformation power curve.

Westinghouse identified resistance as a key factor that creates lower profits for **two to three years after a change has taken place.** They observed, " . . . *the disruptive effect of cultural resistance is longer and more costly than we believed or understood.*" Knowing this, it will be interesting to watch how they handle their recent $5.4 billion takeover of CBS.

We have found the prescription for successful change is proactively involving all stakeholders in the transformation process (leaders, employees, owners, vendors, and customers, etc.). To do this requires a multi-level transformation process.

In the next chapter we identify, define, and recommend a comprehensive multi-level process that focuses on all of the key transformation leverage points and players. Read on...☞

The Unvarnished Truth...

"You can't transform a company of our size with fond hopes and fervent wishes.

It requires a carefully crafted plan based on a vision, and an unbending commitment to carry it out."

--Don Guinn,[15] Former CEO, Pacific Telesis

7

Transformation = Trophy

Transformation equals what? Trophy? Yes, a transformation trophy. The Greeks used the word "trope" to signify a turning point. The early use of the word referred to a monument erected on the exact spot where an adversary was turned back on the battlefield.

In transformation process the adversary is the status quo. Change begins at the point where the seeds of change burst through the cracks in foundation of the status quo and so begin its demise. In order for that to happen, nothing short of total commitment, solutions, actions, and results will do.

Solutions--Actions--Results

No leader or consultant can singlehandedly prescribe the ideal solution for your transformation. The principles are the same for each company, however the uniqueness of each company's strategy, structure, and culture requires a tailored change process.

Creativity, planning, and forward momentum are what make change work. Finding ways to blend them effectively is a mutual responsibility between the leader, the leadership team, the coach/consultant/change agent, and the people closest to the problem, the employees. Collaboration creates the right kinds of solutions that propel the transformation process.

First Things First--Outlaw The Quick-Fix

According to Michael H. Walsh, president, Tenneco Inc., *"As one up to his neck in the challenge of transforming a mature, multi-billion dollar organization, I find it much easier with the support of the entire culture. I've also found there is no such thing as a 'quick-fix,' no easy way to do it."*

Transformation is tough and takes time. Building an adaptive culture requires killing quick-fix approaches and carrying out a long-term change strategy.

An Integrated, Multi-Track Approach

History Lesson--For the past fifty years companies and consultants have focused on narrow single-track processes to transform organizations. Each had a single action lever such as: structural reorganization, management training, team building, strategic planning, design of reward systems, and managing corporate culture. By the early '80s, it was obvious that no single track got the job done.

Now--Today's competitive environment requires a deeper, more effective level of organizational change. Organizations who are committed to change require integrated, multi-track transformation processes which touch everyone and everything in the organization.

Why?--Organizations are truly complex, interconnected systems that require an integrated, multi-track approach involving all levels of the organization's infrastructure. By doing this, all of the key leverage points in the organization are impacted--not just one or two.

Ralph Kilmann, in his book, *Managing Beyond The Quick Fix*, identified how five key leverage points can be addressed by carefully designed and integrated *tracks*.[16] Following is the way we integrate the five tracks:

1. **The Culture Track**: Every organization has an invisible quality--a certain style, a character, a way of doing things--that ultimately determines whether successful transformation will be achieved. The Culture Track is designed to establish trust and information sharing, as well as gauge adaptiveness, receptivity to change, and improvement of the culture.

2. **The Strategy-Structure Track**: Realigning objectives, tasks, and people with the new strategic directions, this track addresses the most important questions confronting the members of the organization: Where are we now? Where are we going? How will we get there? What's in it for us if we help you get there?

3. **The Leadership/Management Skills Track**: This track augments change skills to cope with complexity, exposing and updating assumptions about human change processes. Most leaders and managers have not had a common learning experience together, and this track enables everyone the opportunity to begin the transformation with their toe on the same starting line.

4. **The Team-Building Track**: This track infuses new cultural norms and assumptions into each work unit, fostering cooperative efforts. Team building fully activates both the new culture and the new skills throughout the entire organization. To be effective, it is led by the line managers themselves, who act as examples of the behavioral changes required in the new culture.

5. **The Reward System Track**: Establishing a change-motivating reward system that sustains the whole improvement effort, this track divides rewards into two basic types: intrinsic and extrinsic. Intrinsic rewards are the positive feelings a person gets while performing her/his job. Extrinsic rewards are given formally by the organization and can include increased salary, bonuses, paid vacations, fringe benefits, office furnishings, promotions, etc.

6. **The "Shadow" Track**: Although not one of the formal identifiable tracks of the process, the shadow track is the management of the integrated process. This is the critical piece that communicates to the culture that the transformation is not a fad, or the "program de jour," and keeps the process alive through top management involvement.

Typical Multi-Level Process

The following chart, Figure 6.1, outlines a typical multi-level design and schedule. However, to be effective, every process must be designed to meet the specific needs of the organization, and will have a different pattern for each company.

Figure 6.1

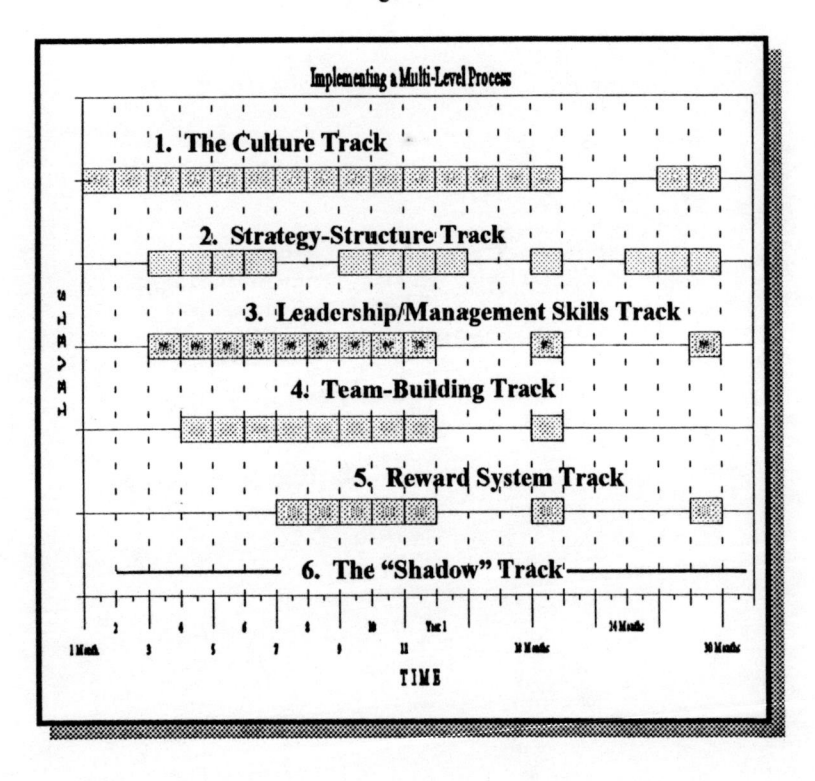

Implementing a Multi-Level Process

1. The Culture Track
2. Strategy-Structure Track
3. Leadership/Management Skills Track
4. Team-Building Track
5. Reward System Track
6. The "Shadow" Track

TIME

"Strangely enough, this is the past that somebody in the future is longing to get back to."

--Ashleigh Brilliant
(also 'Doc' Brown in
Back to the Future)

8
Transformational Leadership

Transformation plumbs the depths of its leaders. It's not a game for lightweights. It demands greater emotional depth than day-to-day operations. Norman Lear, chairman and CEO of ACT III Communications, recommends:

> *"The lofty ideas of 'inspiration' and 'spirit' need to be courageously identified with transformational leaders at a time when other leaders use them with some embarrassment. These ideas are the bedrock of successful transformation."*

The leader is THE "game-maker" in every transformation! Following are the attitudes and attributes we've found essential for leaders embarking on the transformation journey.

The Ten Most Powerful Attributes of Transformational Leaders

Transforming an organization means successfully moving it out of its comfort zone. In addition to the normal day-to-day leadership skills, transformation takes a special set of leadership attributes that unleash the synergistic power of the culture.

✓ **Vision** - Vision is the sine qua non of transformational leadership. Like all great odysseys, transformation can be filled with triumph and defeat, joy and heartbreak. However, it always moves with a sense of something greater to be achieved.

Imagine trying to lead an expedition where you knew where you were going, but the group you were leading wore blindfolds! Not only must you have a clear unshakable vision of what you want to accomplish but commitment to constantly communicate it to all involved.

Vision is very powerful, and the lack of it can lead to defeat. Florence Chadwick is a great example. Having already swum the English Channel both ways, she decided to swim from Catalina Island to the California coast. Here's what happened.

> *It was the morning of the Fourth of July, 1952, the sea was like ice and the fog so dense Florence Chadwick could hardly see her support boats. Against the frigid grip of the sea she pushed on valiantly for sixteen hours.*
>
> *Alongside her in one of the boats, her coach offered encouragement. She began to struggle, and he urged her on. She had never quit before . . . but sadly, with only a half mile to go, she asked to be pulled out.*
>
> *Later, she told a reporter, "Look, I'm not excusing myself, but if I could have **seen** land I might have made it." She had lost sight of her goal.*
>
> *Two months later, however, despite the same dense fog and ice cold water, she swam again, faith intact with a clear picture of her goal in her mind. She triumphed. Florence Chadwick became the first woman to swim the Catalina Channel, eclipsing the men's record by two hours!*[17]

Vision is the most important tool you can use to motivate yourself and your culture to stay on course.

✓ **Commitment** - Obviously, commitment to the vision is vital. Remember Yoda, of "Star Wars" fame, the little green wise man who helped Luke Skywalker? During Luke's trials to master The "Force," Yoda coaches him in a critical moment by saying, *"Try, there is no try. Only do or do not do!"* Transformational leaders are committed "doers" not "triers." They don't start and stop, they stay the course.

Thomas Edison is a great example. In his lifetime he produced more than 1,300 inventions that changed the world. One of Edison's inventions, of course, was the light bulb. In the process, he tried over 2,000 experiments with different techniques and materials before he got it to work. A reporter asked him how it felt to fail so many times. He said, *"Fail? On the contrary, I never failed once. I invented the light bulb. It just happened to be a 2,000-step process."*

Like Edison, transformational leaders commit for the long term. They invest in personal, professional, and organizational development with a passion for success and achievement.

✓ **Gratitude** - Gratitude, sincere and plentiful, is the grease the transformation process slides forward on. Philosopher William James observed, *"The deepest principle in human nature is the craving to be appreciated."*

The hard work and stress of change requires the leader's sharp eyes and ears to actively catch people doing the right things. Thanking them publicly and privately supports the transformation process in deeply personal ways. No effort is too small to recognize.

Acknowledge *the families* of hard working transformers, and find ways to communicate to and appreciate them continuously as well. In fact, reward people who show *appreciation,* and watch the process grow!

Remarkably, one person almost always gets left out. Don't overlook him or her. Remember, to appreciate yourself as well!

✓ **Flexibility** - Flexibility is vital when carrying out the multi-track transformation process. Demonstrating tolerance for ambiguities is a great example for others to follow. And by planning and scheduling the process you align the team and avoid confusion. As the schedule rolls out, senior leaders must constantly adjust their course when they see clues suggesting a change of strategy.

A major part of flexibility is patience. The initial plan never unfolds exactly as originally designed. There are always surprises in a transformation process because human nature does not lend itself to totally predicable paths.

✓ **Integrity** - *"As I grow older, I pay less attention to what leaders say. I just watch what they do,"* said Andrew Carnegie. People look up to their leaders for honest, fair, and straightforward treatment during change. If they think they're being led down the primrose path, they resist, and resistance is the archenemy of change.

In *Hanta Yo*, Ruth Beebe-Hill's book, about a Lakota Sioux leader, she wrote, *"Some will say he is a messenger . . . I say he is the message."* Ken Bertaccini, senior executive at AT&T and a veteran of the largest corporate transformation in the world, put it this way:

> *"You can't fake integrity. Many have tried, and all have failed. When it comes to transforming a business there is no substitute for honesty and integrity. Leadership is the art of getting things done through people, and it won't happen unless they believe in you.*
>
> *You have to be honest and let them know what your goals are--what you want to accomplish, why you want to accomplish it, how they will benefit from it, and the role they will play in accomplishing it.*
>
> *No chief executive, nor top management committee ever reached these goals without integrity. Unless the entire management team and culture is on board, the company will never get there."*

✓ **Healthy Point of View** - A healthy, optimistic point of view is critical to the transformation leader's success. It is contagious, and creates energy and hope.

Becoming healthy can be viewed as a path with principles that act as beacons along the way. Six of these are *generosity, ethics, acceptance, energy, reflection,* and *wisdom.* Keys to healthy leadership, they are, as Warren Bennis says, *"The creative deployment of self."* These principles are the well from which the leader draws out inspiration and spirit for the transformation process.

Another benefit of a healthy point of view is that it helps to moderate both the successes and failures of transformation. Don Shula, head coach of the Miami Dolphins put it this way, *"Failure isn't fatal, and success isn't final."* Does that mean you as a leader are never disappointed and down? No. It just means you don't let it *keep you down*. A healthy point of view gives you the resilience you need to marshal your people towards the long term transformation goals.

✓ **Sense of Humor** - Another football coach, Lavel Edwards, of Brigham Young University, has a reputation of always having a serious face during games. He tells this story about himself when he won the National Championship:

> *"I was asked by a friend if I was happy about winning the championship?" I emphatically answered, "Yes!" The person then chided me a bit and said, "Then why don't you tell your face?"*

A leader's sense of humor communicates in ways words can't. It eases the negative energy around mistakes during transformation. It short-circuits people's tendency to blame others. Does that mean that mistakes are a laughing matter? No. It just means we need to laugh at ourselves instead of beating each other up. The less blame during transformation, the more progress you make.

✓ **Vulnerability** - What, you say, Vulnerability? Yep, vulnerability. One of the problems with the '70s and '80s was the expectation that leaders somehow, someway knew everything and exactly what needed to be done in every situation. It wasn't true then, and it's not true now. So, the way to show it is by being vulnerable.

Transformation requires leaders who are willing to grow. Consider the macho icon of Sir Edmund Hillary:

> *In 1952, New Zealander Edmund Hillary attempted to climb Mount Everest, 29,000 feet straight up. He failed. A few weeks later, he was asked to address a group in England. Hillary walked to the edge of the stage, made a fist and pointed at a picture of the mountain and said in a loud commanding voice, "Mount Everest, you beat me the first time, but I'll beat you next time because you've grown all you are going to grow . . . and I am still growing!"*
>
> *One short year later, on May 29, 1953, Edmund Hillary and his Sherpa climbing partner, Tensing Norgay, became the first men to stand on the summit of Mount Everest.*

Vulnerability makes sense. When you're not sure what to do, if you make a mistake, or in any situation where you can demonstrate that you are human, be vulnerable. Seeking assistance from your team is one of the most empowering actions a transformation leader can do for them.

✓ **Gritty Determination** - In November 1950, during the Korean War, U.S. Marine Corps General Chesty Puller's 1st Marine Division was surrounded by eight divisions of Chinese regulars at the Chosin (Chosgjin) Reservoir. He wryly commented to his staff, *"Well, now we got 'em where we want 'em. They can't get away from us now."* He and his Marines successfully fought their way out of the danger.

Transformation requires determination to overcome roadblocks and detours that inevitably appear on a daily basis. Take the fifty-six signers of the U.S. Declaration of Independence for example:

> *When they signed the Declaration of Independence, they wrote, "For the support of this declaration, with a firm reliance on the protection of the Divine*

> *Providence, we mutually pledge to each other, our lives, our fortunes, and our sacred honor," and they meant it. They signed it knowing full well that the penalty would be death if they were captured.*
>
> *Five of them were captured and tortured before they died. Twelve had their homes ransacked and burned. Two lost their sons in the Revolutionary War, and another had two sons captured. Nine of the fifty-six fought and died from wounds or hardships of the war. One was driven from the bed of his dying wife, and his thirteen children, whom he never saw again.*

Successful transformation = gritty determination.

✓ **Making Success Attainable and Human** - For too long, the myth of superhero leaders has clouded the reality that success is attainable and human. Most of us grew up in an era where the heroine or hero swept in, sized problems up immediately (and was never wrong), solved them, and rode off into the sunset. This truly comes from mythology, and it belongs there.

Transformation is carried out in real life by everyday people committed to extraordinary ideas, fighting uncommon odds to get the job done.

Would you bet that someone without formal art training, who wrote his first book to amuse himself would become a runaway, worldwide best-selling author? Not in today's lightspeed society. But Theodor Geisel did just that:

> *Geisel tried continuously to get someone to print his work. After hundreds of rejections, a close friend published his first book out of pity. The result? He published forty-four books in nearly every language, received a Pulitzer prize and virtually every children's book award--including the Laura Ingalls Wilder Award and three Caldecott Honors. His characters are gleefully reborn again and again as his books are reprinted in the millions and his stories retold in animated television specials.*

"And to Think That I Saw It on Mulberry Street" started it all for Theodor Geisel in 1937 as Dr. Seuss. His last children's book in 1990, *"Oh, the Places You'll Go!"* was on the New York Times bestseller list for over a year.

Dr. Seuss (or maybe it was the "Cat in a Hat") taught us that success is attainable and very human, and we can succeed with a sense of humor.

Is All the Hard Work Worth IT?

"The purest gold and the finest steel has to go through the hottest fire," says an Irish proverb. The twelve successful companies with adaptive, motivated, cultures discussed in Chapter 3 (Figure 3.2) were able to go through the refiners fire because they had transformational leaders who led the way.

Those twelve adaptive companies were committed to all their stakeholders and never gave up. Together with their adaptive cultures they created growth of *682% Revenue, 282% Employment, 901% Stock Price, and 756% Net Income.*

Winston Churchill, a great transformational leader, put it this way, *"Never, never, never, never quit!"*

Myopia Grande

"Everything that can be invented has been invented."

--Charles H. Duell, Commissioner U.S. Office of Patents, 1899[18]

9
Using 'Outsider' Eyes

Ralph Waldo Emerson observed, *"The field cannot well be seen from within the field."* Spotting dynamics of transformation are also hard to see when you're inside the organization. T. D. Weinshall, in an article titled "Help for Chief Executives: The Outside Consultant," eloquently summarizes why leaders cannot transform their organizations all by themselves:

> *"The question is whether leaders need, and can be helped by, outside consultants?. . . The answer is a definite 'yes.'*
>
> *Managements in all organizations suffer from a condition called the 'no-full-disclosure disease.' This ailment manifests itself through people in the management structure who do not reveal their concerns because it may come to the notice of those who affect their position [power] in the organization. They worry about their direct boss, their peers, and their subordinates.*
>
> *The no-full-disclosure condition is a universal one and no organization is free from it. When managers are first told of its universality they are surprised, thinking that it only affects their own organization and themselves.*
>
> *Curing the 'no-full-disclosure disease' and its residual effects can be done only with the assistance of competent outside consultants [outsider eyes]. Consultants help managers to open up [acknowledge reality], bridge the communication gap, and find solutions to the organizations problems. The consultant acts similar to a nautical pilot assisting the captain of a large ship guide it*

safely through a hazardous passage."[19]

Modern leaders aren't the only ones who've been blinded by their immediate environment. Napoleon Bonaparte, one of the world's greatest military tacticians, failed to see how new technology could help his armies. After being approached by Robert Fulton who proposed steam powered warships for his navy, Napoleon rudely dismissed him by saying:

"What, sir, you would make a ship sail against the wind and currents by lighting a bonfire under her decks? I pray excuse me. I have no time to listen to such nonsense."

When leaders realize the world has changed and they no longer should expect themselves to be on top of every situation, this will relieve some of their pressure and encourage them to quickly seek a consultant/coach/change agent with "outsider eyes" to safely guide them through the hazardous transformation process. Imagine what a different world it would be today if Napoleon had done that.

According to James J. Kelly, President, W.T. Grimm & Co., and a veteran of numerous reorganizations, mergers and acquisitions, *"Someone with an outsider's point of view looks beyond the balance sheet to create a successful outcome by meshing the complex people issues of organization transformation."*

Coaching--Key to Transformation

Both leaders and their senior team who are responsible for the restructuring need organizational and one-on-one coaching.

The Need--It's no secret that world-class performers in art, music, dance, literature, and athletics use coaches to direct their development and attainment of higher levels of performance. World-class leaders and teams need world-class coaches. The tougher the competition, the higher quality the coach.

The Reality--Two trends consistently pop up for us when working with senior leaders:

1. As leaders rise higher on the corporate ladder, they often become *too busy to be coaches, and be coached*. Leaders who fail to seek bottom-up coaching for any reason are taking the first, fatal step to losing touch with their people and the "bigger" transformation game.

2. Many people are intimidated or reluctant (afraid) to give leaders coaching. They often excuse themselves by saying their leaders don't want coaching, but in reality, they fear possible negative consequences or repercussions.

In either case, lack of coaching is deadly in the transformation game. One of the highest priorities of leaders is building a "coaching rich" environment throughout the organization. Bill Marré, senior partner in The William Marré Company, a leading edge management consulting firm, has dubbed this, *"Speaking your truth with respect."*

Choosing The Right Consultant/Coach/ Change Agent

Choose a consultant/coach/change agent who will be your "change partner," over the long term. Choose someone who sees your organization **as it is**, who tells you what you **don't want to hear**, and **coaches you as a leader**. Key attributes of a coach are:

✓ **True Partnership** -- Choosing a consultant/coach/change agent is like selecting a new board member--the individual or company must be at your planning table from Day One as a full partner in the development of your transformation strategy.

✓ **Professionals Only!** -- It is definitely not a job for amateurs. Senior leaders need seasoned professionals with successful track records in the organization change arena. The fact is you can't lead others past where you are. You need professionals who bring expertise in building cultures and a well-rounded knowledge of business, have grown themselves, and have the lumps to prove it.

✓ **Ups and Downs** -- Ups and downs are a natural part of the transformation process. Nothing goes flawlessly, and the relationship between you and your consultant/coach/change agent should be so well grounded that it will survive the ups and downs. This, of course, is a mutual responsibility.

✓ **Long Term Relationship** -- Transformation takes time, energy, commitment, and teamwork. It is also tricky business. Transforming an organization into an adaptive, performance-enhancing team requires teamwork and trust between the senior executive and the consultant/coach/change agent.

✓ **Hands-on Business Experience** -- It also takes a consultant/ coach/change agent who understands all the key leverage points of corporate culture, strategy/structure, leadership/management skills, team building, reward systems, and organizational dynamics. Choose one whom you can trust with the most intimate details of your business and who will customize a transformation process to meet your company's unique needs.

Investing In Your Future

There is a lot of banter about the cost of consultants. Many people feel they are expensive. But, expensive compared to what?

Successful transformation takes somewhere between two to five years, and you need a consultant/coach/change agent who will pilot you through the entire process. You need someone who will keep pace with your needs and "be there" when you need them. As the transformation leader:

☞ Expect and demand **weekly contact and coaching** with all the members of your senior team.

☞ Expect and demand **an organization-wide transformation process** which takes you and your consultant/coach/change agent to every location, and literally touches every employee, vendor, customer, officer, and stakeholder before it's over.

☞ Expect a **budget to match** the magnitude of the process. Transformation requires long-term financial and time resources. When it's all said and done, the budget will be small in comparison to the ROI.

Question 1-- *"How much is your organization's collective time worth?"* A consultant/coach/change agent will cut through cultural obstacles and accelerate the accomplishment of your goals.

Question 2-- *"How much is increased profitability and productivity worth?"* A good consultant/coach/change agent will help you maintain profitability in the short term, and *significantly improve* in the long term (See Chapter 3, Figures 3.1 and 3.2).

Where Do You Go From Here?

Well, here we are back where we started, *"Transform now or be transformed later."* Act or be acted on. Move or be moved.

Either you *decide* to transform, or the decision will be made for you. When you *commit* yourself to *act*, your actions make a statement that cannot be misunderstood. William the Conqueror knew this when he launched his successful invasion of England from Normandy in 1066:

> *After landing in England, William unloaded his soldiers and cavalry from the ships that carried them across the English Channel. While his officers and men stood on the beach in shock and disbelief,* **he burned their boats.** *He reportedly said, "We either beat them and return home in their boats, or perish in the attempt." They prevailed over the Saxons at the Battle of Hastings, and he was crowned King William I of England on Christmas Day, 1066.*

We live in the same kind of era. *There is no going back.* It takes commitment, guts, and determination to "burn the boats" and lead the way. What a great opportunity! Hyrum Smith, of *Franklin Planner* fame, is fond of quoting a simple but powerful poem:

> *There is no chance, no destiny, no fate,*
> *That can circumvent, hinder, or control*
> *The firm resolve of a determined soul.*

Now all you have to do is *decide*. . .

...Transform or Be Transformed?

Transformation Note

☑ IF... you've read this far, you're ready for the next set of transformation choices. We would like to help. Give us a call. We can help you put your transformation process "on track." We're experienced, down-to-earth, and fellow travellers with you on the transformation path.

Call us today at **805 549-8246**, or fax us at **805 549-0339**.

☑ IF... you think we're just a little too wacky about this transformation stuff, and you are waiting until you're really sure you need it, no harm done. We hope you enjoyed reading the book and hope you'll pass it on to someone else, or keep it until you need it.

☑ IF... you have suggestions for us, just call or fax to the above numbers. We'd love to hear from you!

Thanks again. The pleasure has been ours . . . . . .

Consultant/Coach/Change Agents

"The management of change requires skill and talent. It requires insight and understanding. It requires the coordinative efforts of knowledgeable change agents to make transformation successful."

--Lee Grossman[20]

10
Seasoned Consultant/Coach/ Change Agents

BRADY & ASSOCIATES
1377 Woodside Drive, Suite 2001
P.O. Box 772
San Luis Obispo, California 93406
Telephone: 805 549-8246
Fax: 805 549-0339
Internet/email: ONEBULLDOG@AOL.COM

🐞

WHEELWRIGHT ASSOCIATES
P.O. Box 221668
Carmel, California 93922
Telephone: 408 624-8138
Fax: 408 624-8138
Internet/email: TIMSMITH@REDSHIFT.COM

The Right Things Get Done:

• *People achieve.*

• *Business gets better.*

• *You get results!*

Our Sources

11
Endnotes

1. Chinese Pictograph, *Wéi Jī*, is made of two parts: "danger" and "opportunity."

2. Peters, Tom.. *The Tom Peters Seminar.* New York: Random House, 1994.

3. Allen, Robert. News Conference on September 20, 1995 as reported by Reuters News Service.

4. Kuhn, Thomas. *The Structure of Revolutions.* New York: Bantam Books, 1964.

5. Cerf, Christopher, and Navasky, Victor. *The Experts Speak.* New York: Pantheon Books, 1984. Reportedly spoken to Karl V. Karlstrom, in response to his recommendation that a manuscript on the new science, circa 1957.

6. Toffler, Alvin. *Powershift: Knowledge, Wealth, and Violence At The Edge of The 21st Century.* New York: Bantam Books, 1990.

7. Gyohten, Toyoo, and Volcker, Paul. *Changing Fortunes: The World's Money and Threat To American Leadership.* New York: Times Books, 1992.

8. Pareto, Vilfredo. *The Mind of Society.* Lausanne, Switzerland: 1916. Pareto (1848-1923), an Italian economist and sociologist, born in Paris, France. He applied mathematics to economic and sociological analysis. Pareto grew up in Italy, graduated from the University of Turin., and became a professor of political economy at University of Lausanne, Switzerland in 1893.

9. Kilmann, Ralph H., Covin, Teresa Joyce, and Associates. *Corporate Transformation.* San Francisco: Jossey-Bass, 1990.

10. Kotter, John P., Heskett, James L. *Corporate Culture and Performance.* New York: The Free Press, 1992.

11. Pritchett, Price *After the Merger: Managing the Shockwaves.* New York: Dow Jones-Irwin, Inc., 1985.

12. Yeomans, William N. *1000 Things You Never Learned in Business School.* New York: McGraw-Hill, 1985.

13. Xicom, Inc. Promotional Brochure, Tuxedo, New York: 1995.

14. Beckhard, R., and Harris, R. *Organizational Transitions.* Reading, Mass.: Addison-Welsey, 1977

15. Pacific Telesis. *Pacific Telesis: 1983 Annual Report.* San Francisco: Pacific Telesis, 1983.

16. Kilmann, Ralph H. *Managing Beyond the Quick Fix.* San Francisco: Jossey-Bass, 1984.

17. Canfield, Jack, and Hansen, Mark Victor. *A 2nd Helping of Chicken Soup for the Soul.* Deerfield Beach, Florida: Health Communications, Inc.. 1995.

18. Morgan, Chris and Lanford, David. *Facts and Fallacies.* Exeter, England: Webb & Bower, 1981.

19. Weinshall, T. D. *Help for Chief Executives: The Outside Consultant.* California Management Review, 1982, *24* (4), 47-58.

20. Grossman, Lee. *The Change Agent.* New York: AMACOM, 1974.

Περι Αἴτιὄς*

*About the Authors

JOHN BRADY—How does a country boy from a remote desert town grow up to become a leading edge thinker, speaker, consultant and author on the subject of change management? By being caught in the clash between the proverbial "immovable object and the irresistable force" as he matriculated through the U.S. Marine Corps and the old Bell System, and then experienced, first hand, the 'train wreck' created by the first AT&T divestiture. After managing the largest successful cultural transformation process in the U.S., John was nicknamed "Bulldog" by his clients and colleagues for his direct, tenacious consulting approach. He is well known for his total commitment to his clients' success. John makes his home in San Luis Obispo, California when he's not in an American Airlines Admirals Club somewhere across the world.

TIMOTHY SMITH—Whats a poet, philosopher, lumberjack, longshoreman doing as a leadership consultant? Sharing the wisdom on living and working effectively that he's gleaned from his encounters with leaders from all walks of life. Tim's vision and practice has grown out of a desire to show individuals and organizations how they can continuously rejuvenate and reinvent themselves. Working with the intangibles that produce 'tangible results', he assists leaders to engage their innate wisdom and common sense to unlock individual, team and organization synergies. Tim excels at helping organizations develop relationships and structures needed to produce, and sustain world-class results. Tim is on a first name basis with all United Airlines employees, and hopes to have a new Boeing 777 named after him. When not flying he makes his home in Carmel, California.